RAPID LEARN JAPANESE SPEECH
IN 7 DAYS OR LESS

EASE YOUR WAY INTO
LANGUAGE

ROBERT ANDERSON

Copyright © 2021 by Robert Anderson
All rights reserved.

No part of this book may be reproduced or transmitted in any form or by any means, electronic or mechanical, including photocopying, recording, or by any information storage and retrieval system without the written permission of the author, except where permitted by law.

Interior Design by FormattedBooks.com

ISBN:

CONTENTS

Introduction vii

Chapter 1	Greetings 1
Chapter 2	Miscellaneous Vocabulary 16
Chapter 3	Travelling 35
Chapter 4	Family & Relationships 44
Chapter 5	Eating Out 54
Chapter 6	Clothes & Shopping 65
Chapter 7	Essential Phrases 74

Answer sheet to quizzes 81
Conclusion 83

A Special Gift To My Readers

Included with your purchase of this book is a copy of my *Crucial Tips & Tricks to Learn Any Language*.

With this you'll receive what I have found over time to be the best practices to ensure you stick to your language goals and also get the most out of your time spent learning.

Click the link below to let me know which email address to deliver it to:

robert-anderson.com

INTRODUCTION

Let's say you're at a sushi restaurant. Your Japanese friend asks you what you're ordering (*nani o tanomimasu ka*). In Japanese, you can say "I am a tuna" (*watashi wa maguro desu*) and it would be a valid answer. Does it sound funny or nonsensical? Without context it would. Say your friend asks you a different question. If your friend asks you; "Which fish do you like: tuna, salmon or mackerel?" Again, you can reply: "I am a tuna" and this would still be valid. How is that possible? In English, you might say "I'm ordering tuna" or "I like tuna", but in Japanese you can get away with what (to us) might be funny-sounding sentences because everything relies on context.

This is just one example of how learning Japanese will be a completely new experience for you. From the way sentences are formed, to how verbs are conjugated (think of the English "speak," "speaks," "spoke" and "spoken"), to which pronoun you should use from a handful of choices—the choice of which will determine whether you are polite, appropriate to the situation or outright rude.

Japanese is not like English. Far from it. It might possibly take you years to achieve fluency. However I hope, just like me, that you would find the beauty of immersing yourself in a whole new language and culture to be rewarding and worth the challenge. We will take it bit by bit, all with example sentences and notes on usage. Sometimes, you will be provided with some exceptions too, so you can avoid embarrassing faux pas.

My name is Robert Anderson. I was born in Scotland. I spent one year in Japan after leaving university and I've fallen in love with Japanese culture and lifestyle ever since. I've been studying Japanese for almost 6 years. I genuinely love languages, and Japanese is one of four that I speak fluently (the others being English, Spanish and Korean). I hope in this book I can share my love of Japanese with others who are interested in learning a gateway to this fantastic culture.

As I've said, I'm not Japanese. However I see this as an advantage. As a second-language learner, like yourself, I believe I can place myself in your shoes and present concepts in a way you will find easy to understand. Whenever I introduce a topic or terminology here, I will try to keep in mind how I would have learnt the same information almost 6 years ago. Am I going too fast? Can I use simpler words? Maybe I can include additional definitions for words that might not be too familiar? These questions and more guided the pace and style of this book.

In all, this book was written with the intention of serving as a good foundation for you to understand basic grammatical concepts and to hold simple conversations. It is unlikely you will be fluent by the time you finish reading this book, but you certainly will have an understanding you can build upon when you, hopefully, decide to dive deeper. Along the way you will find the lessons that you learn here instantly useful as you strike up conversations with new friends, ask for directions, order at a restaurant and so on.

Grammar rules, spelling rules and pronunciation can seem daunting when you encounter them for the first time. A good lesson I have learned by experience is that it's best to just go for it, wing it, and keep trying even if you know you're not being 100% correct. Be confident, but most importantly, have fun!

USING THIS BOOK

The idea with this book is that you do not necessarily have to read it back to front for things to start making sense. You can read the chapter on food and eating out, for example, use the vocabulary and sentences provided and be reasonably well understood right away. With some practise on your pronunciation, of course.

Ideally, you should try to focus on one chapter per day, and then, practise using what you have learned throughout that day!

Example sentences in this book are provided with the Japanese text, the pronunciation of that text and the English translation. Try not to worry too much about the Japanese text right now, I'm not expecting you to learn the couple of thousands of characters used in Japanese—you might be interested to know that Japanese people themselves spend some 12 years of their childhood to master these—in under a week! But it can't hurt for you to become familiar with some, even if that is not the main objective from this book.

There is also an opportunity for you to test yourself in the quiz portion of each chapter. (Relax! It's only one question.)

PRONOUNCING JAPANESE CORRECTLY

Just before we get into our first lesson, we must familiarise ourselves with how Japanese should be pronounced when it is written in the English alphabet. This is important as it will help you sound more native and will also help with how easily you are understood.

All the consonants that you see in this table are pronounced exactly as they normally would be in English. So, "k" sounds exactly like it normally does, so does "h" and so on. You should always keep in mind that the transcription used in this book is phonetic. It means it is written how you should say it (according to a set of rules), but it is more or less consistent, as opposed to English spelling.

Consonants

b - as in **b**all

ch - as **ch**ess. Never pronounced like the French "ch" in words such as **Ch**ardonnay, which sounds like the English "sh."

d - as in **d**og

g - as in **g**et. Always a hard "g," never a soft "g" as in **g**el or colle**g**e. Some speakers pronounce it like the "ng" in si**ng**er.

h - as in **h**ope

j - as in **J**ohn or he**dg**e. Never pronounced like "y" in "Halleluj**a**h" or as a soft "j" as you might find in French words.

k - as in s**k**ill

l - as in fee**l**

m - as in **m**o**m**

p - as in s**p**ot

s - as in **s**ing

sh - as in **sh**ow

t - as in s**t**op

w - as in **w**onder

y - as in **y**es

You might have noticed that this consonant table is missing some letters. Some of those are simply not used when writing Japanese in the English alphabet. However, I've purposely left some consonants out because their pronunciation is a little bit trickier and might require more practise.

- f - You will only find this before the vowel "u" as in Mt. **F**uji or *futari*. The Japanese "f" is a little different from the English "f." While the English "f" is pronounced by passing air between the upper teeth and the lower lip—try pronouncing "f" as you read this—the Japanese "f" is pronounced by passing air between the upper and lower lips. You probably already know how to produce this sound. Think of the word "**ph**ew." Now you don't pronounce it like "few," right?

- n - At the start of syllables, it sounds just like the English "n," but at the end of syllables it sounds more like "ng." But not exactly. It also has the effect of making the syllable that came before it nasal. This is an unfamiliar concept for English speakers but is very familiar for French or Portuguese speakers. The Japanese "n" at the end of words is pronounced with the tongue a little further back than it would be when pronouncing the English "ng." When "n" is before a "k" or "g," it works just like the English "n" in that it turns into an "ng" sound. Think of the word "ba**nk**." Before "b" or "p," "n" is pronounced as "m."

r - The Japanese "r" ranges from being tapped "r" that some English speakers are already familiar with to a tapped "l." Tap refers to the action that your tongue does against the back of the teeth.

ts - I hope this will be the easiest for you to do because we already have this in English. Think of the words ca**ts** or ba**ts**. That's exactly what it is. The only tricky part is it's only found at the end of syllables in native English words, never at the start. Try saying *tsunami*. Are you saying it like <soo-nahmee>? Then, you're not saying "ts" correctly. Try again. It should have that "t" in there.

z - The Japanese "z" actually sounds like "dz." This is not how the English "z" is usually pronounced, but it doesn't mean you aren't already familiar with it. This is the sound in "pi**zz**a." Just like with "ts" though, the tricky part here is pronouncing the Japanese "z" ("dz") at the start of syllables.

Just like with aspiration, the difference with these consonants "f," "n," "ts," "r" and "z" are subtle, and it won't make or break your pronunciation—Japanese people will still likely understand you even if you pronounce these letters as they would be in English, however nailing them are keys to sounding like a native.

Vowels

The vowels are a little more complicated because some Japanese vowels don't sound exactly the same as their English counterparts. In comparison, Spanish or Italian speakers would find Japanese vowels easier to pronounce though as they more closely resemble Spanish or Italian vowels. Listening to recordings would help here.

a - close to but not exactly like the "a" in br**a**

e - sounds like the "e" in l**e**t in Received Pronunciation (standard British English)

i - as in l**ea**ve, m**ee**t or b**ea**t, not like the "i" in b**i**t

o - close to but not exactly like the "aw" in y**aw**n

u - close to but not exactly like the "oo" in b**oo**t. A lot of times it is the unrounded version. It means you will pronounce "u" but without rounding your lips. Many times, it is not pronounced at all. I will note it when this happens, so you don't have to think too much about this for now.

You will occasionally find a bar above the vowels, especially "o" (ō) or "u" (ū). That simply means you should pronounce it twice as long.

When vowels are next to each other, ideally, you should pronounce them just as you would when they are found independently. So, that means "ae" is pronounced like <AH-EH> (without stopping in the middle) not like the "ay" in M**ay**.

Now, without further ado, let's head right to your first day of learning Japanese!

CHAPTER 1
GREETINGS

Naturally, we will get started with greetings. Some people might overlook this topic as too easy and move along, but greetings are of such particular importance in Japanese culture that they basically have their own subset of complex rules you won't find in most other languages. Thankfully, as a second-language learner and as a tourist, you are given extra leeway to make mistakes, but it shouldn't hurt to make your first impression a good one, even if that conversation is only for a while.

SAYING "HELLO"

Let's learn how to say "hello."

Vocabulary

おはよう（ございます）　　good morning
ohayō (*gozaimasu*)

こんにちは *konnichiwa*	hello/good day/good afternoon
こんばんは *kombanwa*	good evening
もしもし *moshi-moshi*	hello (telephone)

Ohayō means "good morning." You can make it polite by adding *gozaimasu* (a lot of times, the "u" is silent, so it sounds more like *gozaimas*). It is best to use polite forms with people you are just meeting and not yet close to. People won't take offense if you leave *gozaimasu* out unless they are your superiors, but as a rule of thumb it is best to use polite forms until you become fluent enough that you can confidently tell when it is appropriate not to be polite.

Konnichiwa is the greeting you will find most useful here. It is equivalent to "hello" or "good day" in English. You can use it in every situation to greet people during the day. You will see that there are two Ns here. Like I said before, Japanese is written here just like how you should pronounce it. So say it like *kon-ni-chi-wa* not *ko-ni-chi-wa*. Make sure you pronounce the double "n" there!

Kombanwa means "good evening." This can be used any time after dark and before sunrise (7 PM to 4 AM typically).

Moshi-moshi is the standard greeting when making or answering a phone call. You don't really use this outside phone calls. (You can do so, but it would sound like you're being sarcastic, like asking if someone is listening. Best not to try this for now.)

The general rule for responding to the above greetings is just saying back what was said to you. So, if someone greets you with *konnichiwa*, you can greet him or her back with *konnichiwa* too!

NICE TO MEET YOU AND FORMING YOUR FIRST JAPANESE SENTENCE

You can also say a stock phrase that is equivalent to our "nice to meet you."

Vocabulary

はじめまして　nice to meet you
hajimemashite

Hajimemashite is a good follow-up after greeting someone for the first time. There are tons of other phrases that range in formality and politeness, but let's keep it simple and stick with this word for now.

Before we forget the vocabulary we've just learned, let's apply them into a sentence.

Example sentence

こんにちは、はじめまして、私はジョンです。

Konnichiwa, hajimemashite, watashi wa Jon desu.

Hello. Nice to meet you. I am John.

We also encountered new vocabulary here.

Vocabulary

私 *watashi*		I/me/my
は *wa*		(topic marker)
です *desu*		am/is/are

Let's focus on the last part of that sentence: *watashi wa Jon desu*. You will notice some things here.

1. Word order - The Japanese word order is always subject-object-verb. This is in contrast with English word order, which is almost always subject-verb-object. When we say "I like cats," Japanese people say "I cats like." In this sentence, we are actually saying "I John

am." This takes some time getting used to, especially when the sentences get more complex and you have to remind yourself to put the verb last.

2. *Watashi* is one of the many first-person pronouns. Just as with some of the words we have learned so far, the reason for this variation is due to differing levels of politeness and formality as well as how high and low you are in terms of social status compared to your listener. Time and time again you will be reminded that word use very much relies on context. But that's a lesson for another time. For now, just remember that *watashi* is I/me/my in English. It doesn't change whether you use it as a subject, object or otherwise, so that's one less thing to worry about!

3. *Wa* - Rather than changing the pronoun itself to show how it is used, Japanese uses different markers. This time we are using *wa* because *watashi* is the topic of the sentence. (Who/what is the sentence talking about?) If you're still wondering why in the very beginning of this book I said you can say "I am a tuna" (*watashi wa maguro desu*) to a friend asking you what you're ordering, it's because *wa* denotes the topic of the sentence (you, the person who is ordering). Although, it is equally valid to translate it as "I am a tuna," a more appropriate translation is "I'm ordering tuna" even if the word "ordering" is not explicitly there. This will come up again and again. Japanese is a contextual

language and Japanese speakers tend to drop information that they assume the listener already knows.

4. *Jon* - It is spelled that way to force your head to read it in a Japanese way as opposed to how you would usually pronounce it. Japanese "John" sounds more like "Jawn" if you can imagine that.

5. *Desu* (often pronounced more like *des*) - This is equivalent to the English "am/is/are." The verb doesn't change depending on whether the subject is in the first/second/third person or whether the subject is singular or plural, but it does change depending on whether… You've guessed it! Whether you're being polite or not. *Desu* is the polite form. You will use it a lot, so be sure to remember it. This is the verb, so it always comes last.

FIRST JAPANESE CONVERSATION

Now that we've talked about the basic sentence structure, let's introduce ourselves some more. This time, we will have our first practise conversation. Maybe you can try figuring out what they are saying on your own using the vocabulary list before heading to the next page where we break them down? Good luck!

Vocabulary

お名前　name
(o-)namae

何　what
nan(i)

か　(question marker)
ka

お元気　well/healthy
(o-)genki

Example sentences

1. おはようございます。はじめまして、私はジェームスです。お名前は何ですか？

    Ohayō gozaimasu. Hajimemashite, watashi wa Jeemusu desu. O-namae wa nan desu ka?

2. お元気ですか？

    O-genki desu ka?

3. 元気です。

    Genki desu.

These sentences also introduce some new concepts, so you're allowed to make mistakes if you happened to take on the challenge of translating them by yourself. You can see the translations below.

Answers

1. **Translation:** Good morning. Nice to meet you. I am James. What is your name?
2. **Translation:** How are you? (Are you well?/Are you healthy?)
3. **Translation:** I'm fine.

So, how did you do? Did you get it all correct? Or were your translations close? If you made some mistakes, that is totally fine. Remember, Japanese is not supposed to be easy. That's why we're taking it very slowly.

FIRST JAPANESE CONVERSATION (BREAKING IT DOWN)

Now, let's discuss new concepts that appeared in these sentences.

Sentence one should be easy enough, but we'll go through it in detail. These are words we have tackled so far, except for the last part: *O-namae wa nan desu ka*? (What is your name?)

I know this might still be tricky for you, but remember in Japanese the topic goes first. What are we talking about in this sentence? What does the question want to know? It's "your name," so that part goes first.

You will notice that there is no word for "your" in this sentence. That is another thing that you will have to get used to. As mentioned earlier Japanese people drop parts of the sentence when it is assumed that the listener already knows what you are talking about. "Your" can be dropped here because of two things.

Firstly, it's a question directed at you. The person asking won't ask what his or her own name is, and they won't ask what some other person's name is when they are clearly talking to you. You can specify "your" name here and make a sentence that explicitly asks for "your" name, but that is not natural for Japanese. The natural way of speaking Japanese is to only provide the necessary information.

The second clue is the use of *o-* (prefix to indicate respect). In Japanese, you use respectful language when referring to other people, but not when referring to yourself. If you did, you would sound boastful. Japanese culture expects people to be humble.

These two are aspects of Japanese that will keep coming up as we progress, so don't worry too much if they are hard to grasp for now. It might be a bit too stereotypical, but what comes to your mind when you hear of Japanese room decoration? Is it minimalism? Japanese people are minimalist in their language too. Again, it's a stereotype, but it's something you can keep in mind when crafting your own sentences.

Finally, we have *nan(i)* and *ka*. *Nani* means what. Many times, it gets shortened to *nan*. I'll explain why and when this happens in later chapters. Meanwhile, *ka* is the question marker. Which means you place it at the end of sentences to turn them into questions. It's that simple. Just keep in mind, when making questions the word order doesn't change. No need to flip words or change their forms as in English. Example: If we turned "Sarah lives in Bristol" into a question, we would get "Does Sarah live in Bristol?" If this were a Japanese sentence, simply adding *ka* makes it a question. Something like "Sarah lives in Bristol *ka*?"

Now, for sentence no. 2 & no.3. *O-genki desu ka?* is a stock phrase that is equivalent to "How are you?" It literally means "Are you healthy?" or "Are you well?" Again, "you" is omitted because we know who we are talking about, and *o-* here means there is respect toward the listener. But notice the response here: *Genki desu* (I'm fine). Besides the omission of

"I" (because we already know you're talking about yourself), you don't use *o-* to refer to yourself.

MORE BASIC CONVERSATION PRACTISE

Let's practise more questions by continuing that conversation.

Vocabulary

あなた *anata*	you	どこ *doko*	where
から *kara*	from	イギリス *Igirisu*	England
来ました *kimashita*	came	歳 *sai*	years old
25(二十五) *ni-jū-go*	twenty-five		

Example sentences

1. あなたはどこから来ましたか？
   Doko kara kimashita ka?
   Where are you from? (Where did you come from?)

2. イギリスから来ました。
   Igirisu kara kimashita.
   I'm from England. (I came from England.)

3. 何歳ですか？
   Nansai desu ka?
   How old are you?

4. 25歳です。
   Ni-jū-go-sai desu.
   I'm 25 years old.

I won't go into more detail regarding these sentences as they are hopefully quite straightforward. Numbers will be covered in tomorrow's chapter.

SAYING "GOODBYE"

Now, it's time to learn how to say goodbye. Goodbyes in Japanese are a little more complicated than saying "hello" because there are several words to choose from (more than are listed here) and the choice depends on context. Unfortunately there is no catch-all word for "goodbye" that you can easily fall back to when unsure of which greeting to use, unlike *konnichiwa* for "hello."

Vocabulary

| おやすみ
(なさい)
O-yasumi
(-nasai) | さようなら
Sayōnara | またね／
また明日
Mata ne /
mata ashita | じゃね
Ja ne | バイバイ
Bai-bai |

O-yasumi(-nasai) is usually translated as "good night" although it literally means "(please) take a rest." Just be sure to use the longer, polite form *o-yasumi-nasai* when saying goodnight to your boss or anyone you're not close to! *O-yasumi* is reserved for family and close friends.

Sayōnara is the actual Japanese word for "goodbye," however people don't really use it, especially nowadays. *Sayōnara* indicates finality, like you're never going to meet that person again, so you're more likely to encounter this expression in TV or film. In real life, not so much. I've even read a survey before that young people don't use it because it makes them feel sad.

Mata ne/mata ashita is the cheerful alternative to *sayōnara*. It literally means "again/tomorrow again." That is to say, you expect to see that other person in the future. (Again, you will notice that the Japanese version is missing some information, because it is assumed that your listener already knows what you're talking about.) When you get better with your Japanese and know the words for time and months, you can replace *ashita* (tomorrow) with the words for next week, next month and so on to tell your listener that you expect to meet them again around that time. *Mata ne/mata ashita* is in no way formal (so you can't use it for business meetings) but it is not rude either, and it is alright to use it with acquaintances whom you are not close to.

Ja ne is an even less formal alternative. I suggest using this once you've become more familiar with your listener.

Baibai (it sounds exactly like "bye-bye") isn't really a proper way to say goodbye, but you will hear it among young women nowadays. I've included it here just to show what lengths Japanese people will go to avoid saying the real word for goodbye.

Quiz

Here we are at the first quiz question! I've tried to construct these in a way that they hopefully summarize some of the main takeaways from what we've just learned, without over-complicating things too much. Try to figure out what this person has just said. You can find the answer sheet at the back of the book (but try to avoid looking at the other answers!)

おはようございます！はじめまして、私はジョンです。あなたはどこから来ましたか？

Ohayō gozaimasu! Hajimemashite, watashi wa Jon desu. Anata wa doko kara kimashita ka?

Did you get it right? Don't beat yourself up too much if you weren't 100% accurate. That was a long day, and we learned lots of new concepts. You can always go back over any parts you found confusing.

The next chapter is going to be dealing with some helpful vocabulary. We're not saying *sayōnara* because we'll meet again tomorrow. *Mata ashita!*

CHAPTER 2
MISCELLANEOUS VOCABULARY

Welcome back! Today in this chapter, we will learn some useful vocabulary, including numbers, telling dates and time, names of the days of the week, names of months, words for the weather and colours. Each of these I felt would be too short to spend a whole day on individually but too important to leave out completely.

JAPANESE NUMERALS

We'll first learn how to count in Japanese.

Numbers in Japanese (1–9)

1	2	3
いち/ひとつ	に/ふたつ	さん/みっつ
Ichi/hito-tsu	*Ni/futa-tsu*	*San/mit-tsu*

4	5	6
し／よっつ	ご／いつつ	ろく／むっつ
Shi/yot-tsu	*Go/itsu-tsu*	*Roku/mut-tsu*

7	8	9
しち／ななつ	はち／やっつ	きゅう／ななつ
Shichi/nana-tsu	*Hachi/yat-tsu*	*Kyū/kokono-tsu*

Japanese numbers are a messy bunch. As you can see, there are two sets for 1 to 9, because they are actually a mix of Chinese (*ichi*, *ni*, *san*…) and native Japanese (*hito-tsu*, *futa-tsu*, *mittsu* numerals. I'll explain how they are different in a while.

Numbers in Japanese (10 onwards)

10	11	12
じゅう	じゅういち	じゅうに
jū	*jū-ichi*	*jū-ni*

13	14	15
じゅうさん	じゅうよん	じゅうご
jū-san	*jū-yon*	*jū-go*

16	17	18
じゅうろく	（じゅうしち） じゅうなな	じゅうに
jū-roku	*(jū-shichi) jū-nana*	*jū-hachi*

19 じゅうに *jū-kyū*	20 にじゅう *ni-jū*	21 にじゅういち *ni-jū-ichi*
24 にじゅうよん *ni-jū-yon*	27 (にじゅうしち) にじゅうなな *(jū-shichi) jū-nana*	30 さんじゅう *san-jū*
40 よんじゅう *yon-jū*	50 ごじゅう *go-jū*	60 ろくじゅう *roku-jū*
70 ななじゅう *nana-jū*	80 はちじゅう *hachi-jū*	90 きゅうじゅう *kyū-jū*
100 ひゃく *hyaku*	**1,000** ひゃく *sen*	

Numbers 10 onwards are generally Chinese numerals. I've written 10, 100 and 1,000 in bold because these are the numerals that you would use to form other numerals. It's a little simpler than counting in English because we don't have to deal with the "teens." If you want to get 11, 10 is *jū* and 1 is *ichi*, so you say *jū-ichi*. Simple! 23 is 2 times 10, so *ni-jū-san*.

As a rule of thumb, when counting with just bare numbers, for example when counting up or down, and you're not counting anything in particular (you're just saying "one, two, three..." not "one person, two persons, three persons..."), then use the Chinese numerals. Now, I did say "generally Chinese numerals" because there are exceptions, notably, 4 and 7. Although they should be pronounced as *shi* and shichi when by themselves, they tend to be pronounced as *yon* and *nana* when combined with other words (i.e., other numerals or counter words). The reason for this is a mystery for most Japanese people and learners alike, but I've been told it's because the Japanese number 4, *shi* is the same word as the word for death; in the case of 7, *nana* is often preferred over *shichi* because it can be easily mistaken as 1 *ichi*.

COUNTER WORDS

If you're counting something in particular, that's when it gets tricky. Unlike in English, you cannot just say "two accountants," "five dolphins" and "190 countries" in Japanese. You have to place counter words either before or after the word you are counting. As English speakers we're lucky that we don't have to deal with this, but it is quite common in Asian languages. However, that doesn't mean it's completely absent from English either. You can't say "three waters" or "11 papers" (unless you're talking about an academic paper or dissertation). You normally have to use a counter word too, like "three cups of water" or "11 sheets of paper," because these words are mass nouns (meaning they are uncountable). This is exactly the same concept in Japanese, except all words are mass nouns, even accountants and dolphins. There are hundreds of counter words and even most Japanese people can't claim to know all of them. In fact, we've already encountered a counter word yesterday. Remember *sai*? That's the counter word for age.

That's where *tsu* comes in handy. It's the counter for when you don't know the counter word for something or if a word doesn't fall under a particular counter word. *Tsu* uses Japanese numerals.

Considering that counter words themselves are quite a complicated topic, it is not really my intention to dedicate an entire lesson to them. However, they are concepts that I think learners should keep in mind for future reference when they learn Japanese numerals for the first time, and I'll include a few more in later chapters that could come in handy for you.

TELLING THE TIME

Time is easy to tell once you already know your way around Japanese numbers. And if you still haven't mastered them, then learning how to tell time is a great way for you to practise!

Vocabulary

時	hour	午前	AM
ji		*gozen*	
分	minute	午後	PM
fun		*gogo*	
秒	second	半	half
byō		*han*	
時間	time		
jikan			

Telling time in Japanese is just like you would in English. You say the hour first, then the minute and finally the second.

One quirk though is AM and PM goes before the time, not after. You are less likely to encounter AM and PM though because Japanese people prefer to use 24-hour notation. For xx hour 30 minutes, Japanese people prefer to use *han* instead of *san-jup-pun*—because isn't *han* so much easier to say? This is pretty much like how we say "it's half past xx" in English.

Wait a minute? Isn't that supposed to be *san-jū-fun*?

Fun actually undergoes a few sound changes when it is paired with certain sounds:

1. 1 minute - いち *ichi* + ふん *fun* → いっぷん *ip-pun*
2. 3 minutes - さん *san* + ふん *fun* → さんぷん *sam-pun*
3. 8 minutes - はち *hachi* + ふん *fun* → はっぷん *hap-pun* (although *hachi-fun* is considered correct too)
4. 10 minutes - じゅう *jū* + ふん *fun* → じゅっぷん *jup-pun*

I've written down some example time expressions below to help you practise.

Example time expressions

1. 午前5時半
   gozen go-ji han
   5:30 AM

2. 午後12時半
   gogo jū-ni-ji han
   12:30 PM

3. 13時41分
   jū-san-ji yon-jū-ippun
   13:41

4. 8時24分
   hachi-ji ni-jū-yon-fun
   8:24

5. 午後10時半
   gogo jū-ji han
   10:30 PM

6. 午前9時3分
   gozen kyū-ji sam-pun
   9:03 AM

7. 11時
   jū-ichi-ji
   11:00

8. 2時5分
   ni-ji go-fun
   02:05

9. 午後1時06分
   gogo ichi-ji roku-fun
   1:06 PM

10. 午前6時半
    gozen roku-ji han
    6:30 AM

TELLING THE DATE

Vocabulary

年 *nen* - year
日 *nichi/ka* - day

月 *gatsu* - month

曜日 *yōbi* - day of the week
月曜日 *getsu-yōbi* - Monday
水曜日 *sui-yōbi* - Wednesday
金曜日 *kin-yōbi* - Friday
日曜日 *nichi-yōbi* - Sunday

週末 *shūmatsu* - weekend
火曜日 *ka-yōbi* - Tuesday
木曜日 *moku-yōbi* - Thursday
土曜日 *do-yōbi* - Saturday

1月 *ichi-gatsu* - January
3月 *san-gatsu* - March
5月 *go-gatsu* - May
7月 *shichi-gatsu* - July
9月 *ku-gatsu* - September
11月 *jū-ichi-gatsu* - November

2月 *ni-gatsu* - February
4月 *shi-gatsu* - April
6月 *roku-gatsu* - June
8月 *hachi-gatsu* - August
10月 *jū-gatsu* - October
12月 *jū-ni-gatsu* - December

昨日 *kinō* - yesterday

今日 *kyō* - today
明日 *ashita* - tomorrow

先週 *senshū* - last week

今週 *konshū* - this week
来週 *raishū* - next week

先月 *sengetsu* - last month

今月 *kongetsu* - this month
来月 *raigetsu* - next month

去年 *kyonen* - last year

今年 *kotoshi* - this year
来年 *rainen* - next year

Japanese months don't have special names. They are just given numbers, so months are relatively easy. Just be careful about April, July and September. They're not *yon-gatsu*, *nana-gatsu* or *kyū-gatsu*. (But note it's *getsu* not *gatsu* when used in expressions like "last month," "this month" and "next month.") Days of the month also have a lot of exceptions of their own, so I am listing them down here. Again, if you're wondering, this mess is because Japanese originally had its own counting system, but it (mostly) got replaced by the Chinese one.

Days of the month

1日	2日	3日	4日	5日
tsuitachi	**futsu-ka**	**mik-ka**	**yok-ka**	**itsu-ka**
6日	7日	8日	9日	10日
mui-ka	**nano-ka**	**yō-ka**	**kokono-ka**	**tō-ka**
11日	12日	13日	14日	15日
jū-ichi-nichi	*jū-ni-nichi*	*jū-san-nichi*	**jū-yok-ka**	*jū-go-nichi*
16日	17日	18日	19日	20日
jū-roku-nichi	**jū-shichi-nichi**	*jū-hachi-nichi*	**jū-ku-nichi**	**hatsuka**
21日	22日	23日	24日	25日
ni-jū-ichi-nichi	*ni-jū-ni-nichi*	*ni-jū-san-nichi*	**ni-jū-yok-ka**	*ni-jū-go-nichi*
26日	27日	28日	29日	30日
ni-jū-roku-nichi	*ni-jū-shichi-nichi*	*ni-jū-hachi-nichi*	*ni-jū-ku-nichi*	*san-jū-nichi*
31日				
san-jū-ichi-nichi				

The Japanese date and time format is always biggest to smallest: YYYY-MM-DD (name of the day of the week) HH-MM-SS. It's not like in English or other languages where you have flexibility whether to say the day first or the month first. It's always biggest to smallest in Japanese. Let's see an example of a full date and time.

2021年4月12日（月曜日）9時15分

にせんにじゅういちねん　しがつ　にじゅうに
にち（げつようび）きゅうじ　じゅうごふん

*ni-sen-ni-jū-ichi-**nen** shi-**gatsu** ni-jū-ni-**nichi** (getsu-**yōbi**) kyū-**ji** jū-go-**fun***

12 April 2021 (Monday) 09:15 AM

Example sentences

Let's try using dates in sentences. Do you still remember *wa* (topic marker), *nan(i)* (what) and *ka* (question marker) that you learned yesterday? We will ask some time related questions based on the date provided on the previous page.

1. 今日は何日ですか?
   Kyō wa nan-nichi desu ka?
   What date is it today?
   今日は12日です。
   Kyō wa jū-ni-nichi desu.
   Today is the 12th.

2. 今日は何曜日ですか?
   Kyō wa nani-yōbi desu ka?
   What day is it today?
   Kyō wa getsu-yōbi desu.
   Today is a Monday.

3. 今は何時ですか?
   Ima wa nan-ji desu ka?
   What time is it now?
   今は午前9時15分です。
   Ima wa gozen kyū-ji jū-go-fun desu.
   *It is no*w 9:15 AM.

("*Nan-ji desu ka*" is similar to "what time is it?")

THE WEATHER

Vocabulary

(お) 天気 *(o-)tenki*	weather	日 *hi*	day
晴れ *hare*	sunny, clear day	晴れています *hareteimasu*	sunny, clear day
雲 *kumo*	cloud, cloudy	雲の日 *kumo no hi*	cloudy, cloudy day
良い *i*	good	悪い *warui*	bad
雨 *ame*	rain	雪 *yuki*	snow
降る *furu*	to fall (down)	が *ga*	(subject marker)
ね *ne*	emphatic marker (isn't it?)	の *no*	genitive marker (of)
どう *dō*	how	でも *demo*	but
もうすぐ *mō sugu*	soon	天気予報 *tenki yohō*	weather forecast

Let's use the above to practise our Japanese some more.

Example sentences with explanation

今日は晴れていますね。
Kyō wa hareteimasu ne.
Today is sunny, isn't it?

Hareteimasu is a verb (to be sunny) whereas English words about the weather tend to be adjectives. Adding *ne* at the end makes your sentence sound softer and friendly instead of sounding authoritative like a news announcer. It's like tag questions in English (isn't it?), but it shouldn't be understood as an actual question. You can be certain that today is sunny and still use *ne*.

今日はお天気がいいですね
Kyō wa o-tenki ga i desu ne.
The weather is good today, isn't it?

今日のお天気はどうですか？
Kyō no o-tenki wa dō desu ka?
How is the weather today?

The reason why *ga* is used in the first but not in the second is that *kyō* ("today") is the topic, and you can think of *o-tenki* ("weather") as a property of *kyō* so it uses *ga* instead. This is a massively oversimplified explanation, and the difference between *wa*, the topic marker, and *ga*, the subject marker, is quite advanced. The rules of when to use which are not something learners should deal with in the first seven days of their study. However, it is impossible to completely avoid using them, even in basic expressions, as they are a part of the sentence structure. So, please just learn these expressions for now. You will get the hang of how to differentiate *wa* and *ga* as you learn more Japanese.

The grammar point that I would like you to remember and understand here is *no*, the genitive marker. That means it tells us that the first word is related to the second word. This relation can be possession, so it is equivalent to the English "of" or "'s" but not always. (Though note that in Japanese it's always <owner> + *no* + <thing owned>.) You might remember, earlier today when we learned how to count, we also used *no* to connect numbers with the words that are being counted. In our example here, it's "today's weather" (*kyō no o-tenki*) that we're talking about. We'll use *no* in the next and last lesson for today too.

> 今日は雲ですね。でも、もうすぐ雨が降りそうです。
> *Kyō wa kumo desu ne. Demo, mō sugu ame ga furisō desu.*
> Today is cloudy. But it looks like it will rain soon.

Kumo just means "cloud" by itself. It might seem weird to us to say something like "today is cloud" if we translate the

Japanese sentence word by word, but this is perfectly acceptable in Japanese.

We place *mō sugu* at the start because it is an adverb of time. *-sō* is a conjugation (verb form) of *furu* ("to fall"), meaning "it seems like." We have to use it for expressions like the weather or hearsay because we don't have control over the weather, and we can only go as far as try to predict it. That's logical, right? In English, we don't really mind when someone says "it's going to rain" like they're certain about it, but Japanese is stricter about this. You only use "will" if you are certain it will happen in the future. If you're not sure and you're only saying it might or you think it will fall, then use *-sō*. You can also replace *ame* with *yuki* to say that snow might fall soon.

Teaching Japanese conjugations is not really the goal of this book. It's a complicated topic, and I think we've dealt with a lot today, so let's end with a rather simple one.

COLOURS

Here are some of the most commonly used colours in Japanese. If you want to use them to describe a word, you can use *no* (colour + *no* + word you want to say has that colour) or using a sentence expression (x is colour y). Some of them can also take an -*i* suffix. In that case, no need to use *no*. You'll see what I mean in the sentence examples after the vocabulary list.

Vocabulary

色 *iro*	colour	白 (い) *shiro(i)*	white
黒 (い) *kuro(i)*	black	緑 *midori*	green
青 (い) *ao(i)*	blue/green	茶色 *cha-iro*	brown
黄色 (い) *ki-iro(i)*	yellow	灰色 *hai-iro*	grey
オレンジ *orenji*	orange	ピンク *pinku*	pink
赤 (い) *aka(i)*	red	紫 *murasaki*	purple/violet

You can place *iro* at the end of these colour words to make it explicit that they are colours, similar to how we can say in English "blue-coloured." In some colour words, having an -*iro* suffix is unavoidable. For example, *cha-iro* (brown) is literally "tea colour" while *hai-iro* (grey) is literally "ash colour."

Ao can mean either green or blue because Japanese people are less strict about the difference. This is why, notoriously, a lot of Japanese traffic lights look blue to outsiders. You can think of *ao* as more of a range between green and blue rather than a point on the colour wheel. *Midori* is the colour if you really want to be strict that something is green and not blue-green.

Example phrases and sentences

白い猫
white cat
shiroi neko

猫は白いです。
The cat is white.
Neko wa shiroi desu.

紫色の花は綺麗です。
The purple flower is beautiful.
Murasaki-iro no hana wa kirei desu.

The choice of using the *-i* suffix or connecting using *no* is generally governed by the following rule: if the colour word can take the *-i* suffix, then using it is preferred. (That doesn't mean you can't use *no*. Using *no* has a different nuance, but let's leave it at that for now.)

I think we've had enough grammar for today, so please concentrate on how the colours were used with the words instead of the verb forms, word order and so on. That is also why I didn't add the new words in the example sentences in our vocabulary list. We'll use them again in a future lesson, but you'll be forgiven if you don't try to remember them this time.

Quiz

You hadn't forgotten about the quiz question had you? It's slightly trickier this time, if you're struggling try having a look back at the vocabulary for help.

時間は午前8時半です。明日は雨が降りそうです。週末の天気予報は何ですか？

Jikan wa gozen hachi-ji-han desu. Ashita wa ame ga furisō desu. Shūmatsu no tenki yohō wa nan desu ka?

Tomorrow, we're going to learn about travelling and places. *Mata ashita. O-yasumi-nasai*!

CHAPTER 3
TRAVELLING

Japan is a beautiful place with many wonderful tourist destinations. I would guess one of the reasons you bought this book is that you want to go to Japan someday to see this fascinating country with your very own eyes. In this chapter, we're going to learn several sentences and words that are related to transportation and getting around in general, including asking for directions to common places and establishments, knowing the basic verbs for movement and many more useful scenarios where you can put your Japanese into practise.

Our vocabulary list is long this time, so I am going to break it down into topical sections. Don't try to memorize them in one sitting. Come back to them for reference as you browse the example sentences, which will comprise the bulk of this chapter. I will interrupt these sentences every now and then when I think you should take note of a certain language concept. That said, a lot of these will be stock phrases that you can use immediately and tweak on your own by replacing words, so we won't be too heavy on the grammar either unlike in previous chapters. (Did I just hear you breathe a sigh of relief?)

Vocabulary

Modes of transportation

飛行機 *hikōki*	aircraft/plane	自転車 *jitensha*	bicycle
自動車 *jidōsha*	automobile	車 *kuruma*	car
船 *fune*	boat/ship	徒歩 *toho*	(on) foot
バス *basu*	bus	タクシー *takushī*	taxi
電車 *densha*	train	地下鉄 *chikatetsu*	underground

Places

| 空港 *kūkō* | airport | 駅 *eki* | (train) station |
| バス停 *basu-tei* | bus stop | バスターミナル *basu tāminaru* | bus terminal |

ホテル *hoteru*	hotel	スーパー（マーケット） *sūpā (māketto)*	supermarket
コンビニ *kombini*	convenience store	（お）店 *(o)-mise*	shop
レストラン *resutoran*	restaurant	銀行 *ginkō*	bank
家 *ie*	house	部屋 *heya*	room
トイレ *toire*	toilet/restroom	公園 *kōen*	park
ショッピングモール *shoppingu mōru*	shopping mall	病院 *byōin*	hospital

Verbs

歩く *aruku*	to walk	教える *oshieru*	to tell/show/teach
すみません *sumimasen*	sorry/excuse me		

Other useful words

近い *chikai*	close	遠い *tōi*	far
時間 *jikan*	time/hour	到着 *tōchaku*	arrival
出発 *shuppatsu*	departure	-行き *-yuki*	heading (to)
いくら *ikura*	how much	まで *made*	until/up to
道 *michi*	way		

We're going to go through a rather long series of example sentences, so I've also grouped them into situations.

Example sentences - At the airport

1. 空港はどこですか？
   Kūkō wa doko desu ka?
   Where is the airport?

2. 空港がどこにあるのかを地図で教えてください。
   Kūkō ga doko ni aru no ka o oshiete kudasai.
   Please tell me where the airport is on the map.

3. すみません。<u>空港</u>へ行く道を教えてください。／空港へ行く道を教えてくださいませんか？

    Sumimasen. <u>Kūkō</u> e iku michi o oshiete kudasai. / <u>Kūkō</u> e iku michi o oshiete kudasaimasen ka?

    Excuse me. Please tell me the way to the <u>airport</u>. / Could you please tell me the way to the <u>airport</u>?

4. すみません。<u>飛行機</u>の到着時間を教えてください。／飛行機の到着時間を教えてくださいませんか？

    Sumimasen. <u>Hikōki</u> no tōchaku jikan o oshiete kudasai. / <u>Hikōki</u> no tōchaku jikan o oshiete kudasaimasen ka?

    Excuse me. Please tell me the <u>plane</u>'s arrival time. / Could you please tell me the <u>plane</u>'s arrival time?

The difference between *kudasai* and *kudasaimasen ka* is that the former is a command while the latter is a question. Asking a question is more polite than giving a command of course, but they're both useful and totally okay to use. You can also be more specific by replacing *hikōki* with your flight number. (Do you still remember how to count?) I have underlined the words that you can replace to easily make your own sentences.

Example sentences - At the train station

1. <u>駅</u>はどこですか？

    <u>Eki</u> wa doko desu ka?

    Where is the <u>train station</u>?

2. すみません。駅へ行く道を教えてくださいませんか？

   Sumimasen. Eki e iku michi o oshiete kudasaimasen ka?

   Excuse me. Could you please tell me the way to the station?

3. すみません。電車の到着時間を教えてくださいませんか？

   Sumimasen. Densha no tōchaku jikan o oshiete kudasaimasen ka?

   Excuse me. Could you please tell me the train's arrival time?

Example sentences - At the bus terminal

1. 仙台市までいくらですか？

   Sendai-shi made ikura desu ka?

   How much (is the ticket) to get to Sendai City? (How much does it cost to get to Sendai City?)

2. バスに乗ります。

   Basu ni norimasu.

   I will ride a bus.

3. この<u>バス</u>はどこまで行きますか？
   Kono basu wa doko made ikimasu ka?
   What is this bus's last stop? / How far does this bus go? (Literally, "Until where is this bus going?")

Examples sentences - Getting around town

1. <u>ジョージアホテル</u>に行きます。
   Jōjia Hoteru ni ikimasu.
   I'm going to the <u>Georgia Hotel</u>.

2. <u>銀行</u>はどこですか？
   Ginkō wa doko desu ka?
   Where is the <u>bank</u>?

3. <u>自転車</u>を借りれるお店がどこにあるのかを教えてくださいませんか？
   <u>Jitensha</u> o karireru o-mise ga doko ni aru no ka o oshiete kudasaimasen ka?
   Can you tell me where I can rent a <u>bike</u>?

4. おはようございます！最寄りの<u>スーパー</u>はどこですか？歩くかバスに乗るかどちらがいいですか？地図で教えてくださいませんか？
   Ohayō gozaimasu! Moyori no sūpā wa doko desu ka? **Aruku ka basu ni noru ka dochira ga ī desu ka?** *Chizu de oshiete kudasaimasen ka?*

Good morning! Where is the nearest <u>supermarket</u>? **Should I walk or ride a bus?** Can you show me on a map?

(Take note of the sentence in bold. It's a little advanced for now, so we will come back to it in Chapter 5 where we will discuss in more detail how to make questions with choices.)

5. すみません。最寄りの<u>病院</u>はどこですか？<u>病院</u>は車で<u>何分</u>ですか？

    Sumimasen. Moyori no <u>byōin</u> wa doko desu ka? <u>Byōin</u> wa <u>kuruma</u> de <u>nam-pun</u> desu ka?

    Excuse me. Where is the nearest <u>hospital</u>? <u>How many minutes</u> will it take to go to the <u>hospital</u> by <u>car</u>?

6. 最寄りの<u>銀行</u>は<u>タクシー</u>で<u>何分</u>ですか？

    Moyori no <u>ginkō</u> wa <u>takushī</u> de <u>nam-pun</u> desu ka?

    <u>How many minutes</u> will it take to go to the nearest <u>bank</u> by <u>taxi</u>?

7. <u>青森</u>は<u>電車</u>で<u>何時間</u>ですか？

    <u>Aomori</u> wa <u>densha</u> de <u>nan-jikan</u> desu ka?

    How many <u>hours</u> will it take to go to <u>Aomori</u> by <u>train</u>?

Quiz

It's that time again! Try to figure out what this person has just asked:

最寄りの駅はどこですか？駅は徒歩で何分ですか？
Moyori no eki wa doko desu ka? Eki wa toho de nam-pun desu ka?

So, that was a lot of example sentences today and not much grammar for a change. How are you finding the pace? If you find today's lessons too short, you can practise some more by making your own sentences - mix and match words depending on what you have in mind. Remember to practise what you have learned each lesson and try to implement it into the rest of your day where possible! Tomorrow we're going to encounter a lot of new vocabulary related to family and relationships. *Mata ashita!*

CHAPTER 4
FAMILY & RELATIONSHIPS

Today's chapter is going to be rather heavy on the vocabulary side. Since these are specific words for family members, acquaintances, friends and so on, there is really no way of getting around it but to memorize them.

JAPANESE FAMILY TREE (NEUTRAL)

おばあさん *o-bā-san*	grandmother	おじいさん *o-jī-san*	grandfather
おばさん *oba-san*	aunt	おじさん *oji-san*	uncle
母 *haha*	mother	父 *chichi*	father
姉 *ane*	older sister	兄 *ani*	older brother

Rapidly Learn Japanese Speech in 7 Days or Less

妹 *imōto*	younger sister	弟 *otōto*	younger brother
姪 (っ子) *mei(-kko)*	niece	甥 (っ子) *oi(-kko)*	nephew
妻 *tsuma*	wife	夫 *otto*	husband
娘 *musume*	daughter	息子 *musuko*	son
いとこ *itoko*	cousin	孫 *mago*	grandchild

Note: The only difference between the words for grandmother, grandfather, aunt and uncle are the vowel length. (The words for grandparents have a longer second vowel.) This is where it is important to pronounce these words correctly, as it can easily lead to confusion.

This is how you refer to your own family members, however when discussing someone else's family, you will use a different (respectful) word altogether. These respectful words are also how you address your own family members (e.g., when talking to your own sister) unless they're younger than you.

If you were to get married, that makes things more complicated because you would have to learn a whole new set of words for your in-laws. We're not going to discuss in-laws now or the topic would become more complicated than it needs to be. If you really want to talk about your in-laws, you can settle for *tsuma no haha-oya* ("my wife's mother"), *otto no chichi-oya* ("my husband's father") and so on. Japanese people will understand you even if you don't use the exact words. In-law words are quite complicated and even some Japanese people don't know them completely, so they also sometimes settle for "my wife's mother" and so on.

JAPANESE FAMILY TREE (RESPECTFUL)

おばあさん *o-bā-san*	grandmother	おじいさん *o-jī-san*	grandfather
おばさん *oba-san*	aunt	おじさん *oji-san*	uncle
お母さん *o-kā-san*	mother	お父さん *o-tō-san*	father
お姉さん *o-nē-san*	older sister	お兄さん *o-nī-san*	older brother
妹さん *imōto-san*	younger sister	弟さん *otōto-san*	younger brother
姪(っ子)さん *mei(-kko)-san*	niece	甥(っ子)さん *oi(-kko)-san*	nephew
奥さん *oku-san*	wife	ご主人 *go-shujin*	husband
娘さん *musume-san*	daughter	息子さん *musuko-san*	son

いとこさん	cousin	孫さん	grandchild
itoko-san		*mago-san*	

Phew! I know that's complicated, and you've probably noticed that this is a recurring pattern in Japanese now. Japanese people, why do you do this to yourselves?

The reason for this all boils down to respect. The rule of thumb is, when you talk about yourself or your family members to other people (people outside your family), you use neutral words; when you talk about other people or their family members, you use respectful words.

The exceptions here are the words for your uncles, aunts and grandparents. (It wouldn't be Japanese if there were no exceptions after all!) You use respectful words for those regardless of whether they're your family members or other people's family members or you're directly addressing them. The easy explanation here is that they're all older than you, so you have to respect them whatever the case may be.

If you're directly addressing your own family member and they're older than you, use respectful words; if they're younger than you, you may address them by their name. (Addressing people older than you just by their name is rude in Japanese.) I assume most readers aren't going to talk to their own family members in Japanese, so let's just focus on differentiating between your own family members versus other people's family members.

Finally, you will notice that for most of the words, the suffix *-san* is added to make them polite. This is also the same suffix that you add when referring to other people by their name (but not to yourself).

Example sentences

For the following sentences, imagine you are talking with your friend, Yoko, and you're curious to know her brother's occupation. These example sentences are merely for demonstrating the difference between the neutral forms that you use when talking about yourself and respectful forms when talking about others. So, we won't be breaking down the grammar here as we did in previous chapters even though the sentences here are relatively more complicated.

自分：お兄さんはどんなお仕事をされてますか？
Jibun: *O-nī-san wa donna o-shigoto o sareteimasu ka?*
You: What does your brother do?
洋子：兄は銀行で働いています。
Yōko: *Ani wa ginkō de hataraiteimasu.*
Yoko: My brother works at a bank.

Note that in these sentences, we didn't explicitly use the Japanese word for "your" or "my", yet it is still completely obvious (to Japanese people at least) whose relative we are talking about. How is that? It's through the use of respectful words. If you remember our first day's lesson in Chapter 1, this was also the same case with *o-namae* (respectful) and *namae* (neutral). We didn't have to explicitly say "your name" or "my name" in Japanese because this was already implied by how we used respect. If there is respect, then you must be talking about your listener's name and not yourself. It's the same concept here.

Let's learn a few more useful words about relationships. After the following vocabulary list, we will have a few sample sentences that you can use to talk about family, friends and so on.

Vocabulary

独身 *dokushin*	single	結婚しています *kekkon-shiteimasu*	married
離婚しています *rikon-shiteimasu*	divorced	婚約しています *kon'yaku-shiteimasu*	engaged
彼氏 *kareshi*	boyfriend	彼女 *kanojo*	Girlfriend

Example sentences

1. 妹の名前はエリカです。
   Imōto no namae wa Erika desu.
   My younger sister's name is Erica.

2. 私は独身です。
   Watashi wa dokushin desu.
   I am single.

3. 私は結婚しています。
   Watashi was kekkon-shiteimasu.
   I am married.

4. 私は離婚しています。
   Watashi was rikon-shiteimasu.
   I am divorced.

5. 私は婚約しています。
   Watashi wa kon'yaku-shiteimasu.
   I am engaged.

6. 私は彼氏がいます。
   Watashi wa kareshi ga imasu.
   I have a boyfriend.

7. 10年結婚しています。
   Jū-nen kekkon-shiteimasu.
   We've been married for 10 years.

Note: In sentence no. 6, you can replace "boyfriend" with any other person to make your own sentences (e.g., "I have a brother"), but not inanimate objects (e.g., "I have a bag"). You can only use the verb *imasu* with people and animals. If you want to say that you have something, you must use the verb *arimasu* instead. Anyway, let's not get ahead of ourselves.

COUNTING PEOPLE

This might seem weird to put in here. After all, we've already discussed how to count in a previous chapter. But like I said, counting in Japanese is not straightforward. Each word has its own counter word, and in a handful of those counter words which numeral to use can get quite confusing because it's a mix of both native Japanese and Chinese-derived numerals.

To count people, there are special words for one person and two people, while anything higher than that uses Chinese numerals.

1人 - *hitori* - one person   5人 - *go-nin* - five people
2人 - *futari* - two people   10人 - *jū-nin* - ten people
3人 - *san-nin* - three people 100人 - *hyaku-nin* - one hundred people

We're learning how to count people now because this will be useful in the next set of example sentences.

Example sentences

1. 兄弟は何人いますか？
   Kyōdai wa nan-nin imasu ka?
   How many siblings do you have?

2. 私は兄が2人、妹が1人います。
   Watashi wa ani ga futari imasu, imōto ga hitori imasu.
   I have two older brothers and one younger sister.

Quiz

That's right! Another quiz question before we end the day. Try figuring out what this person has just said:

私は兄が1人、妹が2人います。兄の名前はピーターです。彼は30歳です。

Watashi wa ani ga hitori, imōto ga futari imasu. Ani no namae wa Pītā desu. Kare wa san-jū-sai desu.

That's all for today! I hope today's lesson wasn't too hard since we didn't cover a lot of grammar. Using respectful words (and when not to use them) was perhaps the tricky part, but it shouldn't be if you just remember the rule: use neutral words when talking about yourself and be respectful when talking about others. This is a concept that will be applicable far beyond just words for family, and will be useful to remember as you continue learning after this book.

But like I said, that's all for today, so before I get carried away with the explanations again, *o-yasumi nasai* and *mata ashita*!

CHAPTER 5
EATING OUT

Japanese is probably my favourite food. Some people who love Japan might say they don't like anime or Japanese music, and some might say they don't know anything about Japanese history. But I have yet to meet a single person who has been to Japan and said they didn't enjoy the food. Japanese food is more than just raw fish and rice. It is an entirely new culinary world—a world that you can explore more deeply by knowing how to speak Japanese.

In this chapter, we will study a few grammatical concepts that will be useful when ordering and asking for recommendations, in addition to words for food, eating utensils, tastes etc. Try not to get too hungry!

CHOOSING BETWEEN X, Y, Z...

One of the sample sentences in Chapter 3 was:

歩くか バスに乗るか　　　どちらがいいですか？
Aruku ka basu ni noru ka　　　*dochira ga ī desu ka?*
Should I walk or ride a bus?

I wrote them in bold letters back then because I said we would come back to it in Chapter 5. And here we are. We'll break this sentence down because this expression is incredibly useful when asking for recommendations, not only for food but also directions, movies and anything really that involves choices.

As you can see, I've separated parts of the sentence, so you can easily distinguish them. The first part is the choices. They can be any number of choices and are separated by the *ka*. The last part is the set phrase. For our purposes now, this is *dochira ga ī desuka* ("Which is better?"). When you get more familiar with this construction, you can replace *i* ("good") with other adjectives, like the Japanese words for "delicious" or "sweet." Let's learn some new Japanese words so we can apply this concept.

Vocabulary

どちら *dochira*	which	お勧め *o-susume*	recommended
美味しい *oishī*	delicious	甘い *amai*	sweet
塩っぱい *shoppai*	salty	酸っぱい *suppai*	sour
苦い *nigai*	bitter	辛い *karai*	spicy
魚 *sakana*	fish	(お)肉 *o-niku*	meat
マグロ *maguro*	tuna	サーモン *sāmon*	salmon
天ぷら *tempura*	tempura	ハンバーガー *hambāgā*	hamburger
スープ *sūpu*	soup	デザート *dezāto*	dessert
スターター *stātā*	starter	メインコース *mein kōsu*	main course
パン *pan*	bread	チョコレート *chokorēto*	chocolate
フルーツ *furūtsu*	fruits	野菜 *yasai*	vegetables
ベジタリアン *bejitarian*	vegetarian	ヴィーガン *bīgan*	vegan

メニュー *menyū*	menu	料理 *ryōri*	cuisine/food
(お)寿司 *(o-)sushi*	sushi	では *dewa*	so/well then
あります *arimasu*	have	ありません *arimasen*	do not have
いかが *ikaga*	how (polite)	(お)飲み物 *(o-)nomi-mono*	drink/beverage
(お)茶 *(o)-cha*	tea	コーヒー *kōhī*	coffee
ジュース *jūsu*	juice	ミルク *miruku*	milk
(お)酒 *(o-)sake*	alcohol	牛乳 *gyūnyū*	cow's milk
(お)水 *(o)-mizu*	water	お願いします *o-negai-shimasu*	I request (please give me).
席 *seki*	seat	テーブル *tēburu*	table
用 *-yō*	for	杯 *hai*	glass
(お)皿 *(o)-sara*	dish/plate	(お)椀 *(o)-wan*	bowl
ナイフ *naifu*	knife	フォーク *fōku*	fork
スプーン *supūn*	spoon	(お)箸 *(o-)hashi*	chopsticks

(お) 会計 *(o)-kaikei*	bill	ください *kudasai*	Please give me
はい *hai*	yes	いいえ *īe*	no
どうぞ *dōzo*	Here you go.	ありがとう (ございます) *arigatō (gozaimasu)*	thank you
と *to*	and		

The vocabulary list is a little longer this time, but don't worry. Most of these are provided so you can have an inventory of words that you can use in your own situations. Thankfully, a lot of them are English-derived, so they should not be too hard to remember. We'll explain some of these words in more depth later in this chapter.

Example sentences

Imagine the following sentences as a conversation between you and a waiter at a restaurant.

1. すみません。メニューをください。
   Sumimasen. Menyū o kudasai.
   Excuse me. Please give me the menu. (May I have the menu please?)

2. はい、どうぞ。
   Hai, dōzo.
   Okay, here you go.

3. ベジタリアン料理がありますか？
   Bejitarian ryōri ga arimasu ka?
   Do you have vegetarian dishes?

4. すみません。ベジタリアン料理はありません。
   Sumimasen. Bejitarian ryōri wa arimasen.
   I'm sorry. We don't have vegetarian dishes.

5. では、マグロかサーモンかどちらがお勧めですか？
   Dewa, maguro ka sāmon ka dochira ga o-susume desu ka?
   Well then, which do you recommend: tuna or salmon?

6. サーモンがお勧めです。美味しいですよ！では、サーモンになりますか？
   Sāmon ga o-susume desu. Oishī desu yo! Dewa, sāmon ni narimasu ka?
   We recommend salmon. It's delicious! So, will it be salmon then?

7. はい、サーモンをお願いします。
   Hai, sāmon o o-negai-shimasu.
   Yes, the salmon please. (Yes, please give me salmon.)

8. お飲み物はいかがですか？
   O-nomi-mono wa ikaga desu ka?
   How about the drinks?

9. お飲み物はお水をお願いします。
   O-nomi-mono wa o-mizu o o-negai-shimasu.
   Please give me water as my drink.

Then after you're done eating.

10. お会計ください。
    O-kaikei-kudasai.
    Please give me the bill. (I would like to have the bill.)

DŌ VS *IKAGA*

If you still remember *dō* from an earlier chapter, *dō* also translates to "how" and in all cases *dō* and *ikaga* are interchangeable. The only reason why a waiter would normally ask "*ikaga desu ka*" instead of "*dō desu ka*" is they have to be polite to customers. The sentence below would be used when asking a friend who is seated at the same table.

> デザートはどうですか？甘いですか？
> *Dezāto wa dō desu ka? Amai desu ka?*
> How is the dessert? Is it sweet?

COUNTING SEATS

As you are aware by now, counting in Japanese is not straightforward. Each thing has its own counter. For most foods, *tsu* is the counter you will use. There are many exceptions, but let's try to keep it simple. Rather, in this chapter we will focus on counting seats (useful when making a reservation or asking for availability) and glasses of drinks.

Seki is the word for "seat", and it is also the counter word for seats. However, we don't need to learn how to count seats themselves at this point. You already know how to count people, right? Look at the following conversation.

> ウェイター：いらっしゃいませ！何名様ですか？
> *Weitā: Irasshaimase! Nan-mei-sama desu ka?*
> Welcome! How many in your party?

> 自分：3人です。
> *Jibun: San-nin desu.*
> Three people.

What the waiter said is a set phrase, so we won't be breaking it down here. It is not something that I expect you will use, but it is something you should be familiar with because this is something they might use with you.

Alternatively, you can use the suffix -*yō* (meaning "for") with the counter for people. Look at the following phrases.

1. 4人用の席
   Yon-nin-yō no seki
   Seats for four

2. 3人用のテーブル
   San-nin-yō no tēburu
   Table for three

Do note that this -*yō* suffix is not a universal equivalent for the English word "for," so you can't just go and translate all your English sentences that have "for" with -*yō*.

COUNTING DRINKS

Drinks are a little more difficult because there is no getting around them. The counter for drinks is *hai*. It uses Chinese numerals except for "four glasses" and "seven glasses," and you need to watch out for those numerals that undergo sound changes with *hai*.

1杯 - *ip-pai* - one glass   2杯 - *ni-hai* - two glasses
3杯 - *sam-bai* - three glasses 4杯 - *yon-hai* - four glasses
5杯 - *go-hai* - five glasses   6杯 - *rop-pai* - six glasses

7杯 - *nana-hai* - seven glasses   8杯 - *hachi-hai* - eight glasses
9杯 - *kyū-hai* - nine glasses   10杯 - *jup-pai* - ten glasses

Example sentences

Now that we have learned how to count seats and drinks, let's try asking the kind waiter again if he can find seats for you and your friend and maybe some drinks too.

1. すみません。2人用の席がありますか？
   Sumimasen. Futari-yō no seki ga arimasu ka?
   Excuse me. Do you have seats for two?

2. お茶を2杯ください。
   O-cha o ni-hai kudasai.
   Please give us two glasses of tea. (We would like to order two glasses of tea.)

Quiz

It's time to apply what we have learned so far. Try figuring out what is being said in the following Japanese sentence. Some of the words might seem too advanced but remember that all the vocabulary has been provided already. So, you can go back to our previous lessons if necessary.

すみません。お飲み物はコーヒーとミルク、スターターはパン、メインコースはお寿司をください。

Sumimasen. O-nomi-mono wa kōhī to miruku, sutātā wa pan, mein kōsu wa o-sushi o kudasai.

Remember, *wa* is the topic marker, meaning the word before it is the topic of that clause.

That is the end of the chapter. We've taught some new grammatical concepts here, especially how to make a multiple-choice question and how to count certain types of words. These will come in handy tomorrow in our next chapter about shopping and clothes. *Mata ne!*

CHAPTER 6
CLOTHES & SHOPPING

You've satisfied your appetite, so now it's time for some shopping. In this chapter, we'll learn the most common words for types of clothing, how to count certain types of clothing and how to ask for prices and recommendations.

Vocabulary

ジャケット *jaketto*	jacket	セーター *sētā*	jumper/sweater
Tシャツ *tī-shatsu*	t-shirt	ズボン *zubon*	trousers/pants
靴下 *kutsu-shita*	socks	靴 *kutsu*	shoes
ワイシャツ *wai-shatsu*	(dress)shirt	ネクタイ *nekutai*	tie
スーツ *sūtsu*	suit	スカート *skāto*	skirt

ワンピース *wam-pīsu*	dress	ジーンズ *jīnzu*	jeans
帽子 *bōshi*	hat	手袋 *te-bukuro*	gloves
新しい *atarashī*	new	古そう *furusō*	looks old
小さな *chīsa na*	small	メディアム *mediamu*	medium
大きな *ōki na*	big/large	サイズ *saizu*	size
安い *yasui*	cheap	高い *takai*	expensive
価格／値段 *kakaku/nedan*	price	現金 *genkin*	cash
ちょっと *chotto*	a little/bit/quite	クレジットカード *kurejitto kādo*	credit card
買う *kau*	to buy	探す *sagasu*	to search/look for
もっと *motto*	more	支払う *shi-harau*	to pay
使う *tsukau*	to use		

A great majority of these words are English-derived or -influenced, so these should be relatively easy to remember compared to previous vocabulary.

Example sentences

Since these sentences introduce some new grammatical concepts and there are lots of opportunities for you to craft your own sentences based on them, we'll spend more time explaining them than we did in the previous chapters. I've also underlined parts of the sentence that you can easily replace with your own.

1. 新しい靴を買いたいです。
   Atarashī kutsu o kaitai desu.
   I would like to buy new shoes.

Just like in English, the adjective is placed here before the word you want to describe.

2. 白いシャツを探しています。
   Shiroi shatsu o sagashiteimasu.
   I am looking for a white shirt.

Do you still remember the colours in Japanese? It would be useful to review them in Chapter 2, so you can practise different sentences.

Also remember the sentences we learned yesterday that you can use at the restaurant? You can also use them today here at the store to ask for recommendations and to ask multiple-choice questions. Let's start with the simplest one.

3. どちらがお勧めですか？
   Dochira ga <u>o-susume</u> desu ka?
   Which do you <u>recommend</u>?

4. もっと小さなサイズのTシャツがありますか？
   <u>*Motto chīsa na*</u> *saizu no <u>tī-shatsu</u> ga arimasu ka?*
   Do you have a <u>T-shirt</u> in a <u>smaller</u> size?

Motto means "more." You place it in front of the adjective that you want to affect. You can change "*motto chīsa na*" with any size you want. "*Ga arimasu ka*" is how you ask "is there…?" or "do you have…?" You place it at the end.

5. 大きなサイズのワイシャツがありますか？
   <u>*Ōki na*</u> *saizu no <u>wai-shatsu</u> ga arimasu ka?*
   Do you have a <u>shirt</u> in a <u>large</u> size?

6. あの靴下はちょっと古そうですね。
   Ano <u>kutsu-shita</u> wa <u>chotto furusō</u> desu ne.
   Those socks <u>look quite old</u>.

7. それはちょっと高いですね。
   Sore wa chotto takai desu ne.
   That's quite expensive.

Now, you need to be careful about sentences 6 and 7 as some shopkeepers might take it negatively. It would help to soften your expression with *chotto* (meaning, "a little" or "quite") and end it all with *ne* (which if you still remember is the emphatic marker to make your sentences sound friendlier and less imposing).

8. もっと安いのはありますか？
   Motto yasui no wa arimasu ka?
   Do you have something cheaper?

9. 現金で支払います。
   Genkin de shi-haraimasu.
   I will pay by cash.

10. クレジットカードは使えますか？
    Kurejitto kādo wa tsukaemasuka?
    Can I use a credit card? (Do you accept credit cards?)

Robert Anderson

COUNTING CLOTHES

Personally, I've seen lots of foreigners go into stores, say *hito-tsu*, *futa-tsu* and so on (the wrong counter words) and get what they want to buy just fine. Shopkeepers will understand you, of course, and chances are they even know English numbers. But that's not why you're studying Japanese, right? So, let's take on the challenge head on!

All the following counter words take Chinese numerals. Just be careful with the inconsistencies in how the counters are pronounced. For example, 4 *mai* is *yon-mai*, but 4 *soku* is *shi-soku*. It won't be Japanese after all if there aren't exceptions on top of exceptions!

枚 ***Mai*** – This is the general counter word for flat and thin things (including clothes). But this counter word is especially useful because you can also use it with other words like sheets of paper and CDs. (If you fold a hat flat, you can count it with *mai*.) But cylindrical, stick-like objects however flat and thin are not counted with *mai*. They have their own counter word. There is a specific counter for clothes that does not apply to other flat and thin things, but since that is less useful let's keep it simple and stick with *mai* when counting clothes, for now. (Likewise, things that come in pairs like gloves also have their own counter word but using *mai* for pairs of gloves works just fine.)

1枚 *ichi-mai*   4枚 *yon-mai*   7枚 *nana-mai*
2枚 *ni-mai*   5枚 *go-mai*   8枚 *hachi-mai*
3枚 *san-mai*   6枚 *roku-mai*   9枚 *kyū-mai*
                                10枚 *jū-mai*

個 **Ko** – This is the counter word that is the closest translation to the word "piece." It is a catch-all for words that do not fall under other counter words, much like the *tsu*. The general rule of thumb is you can use *ko* if the object can be held in the hand, it is not particularly thin or long, and it doesn't fall under any other counter words. I know that's not a very helpful description, but you can just count this as another complexity of the Japanese language. Hats, boxes and balls are counted using *ko*, but pencils are not counted using *ko* because they are long and cylindrical. Mobile phones can be held in the hand, but they are generally counted using the counter word that is used for machinery and devices.

1個 *ik-ko*   4個 *yon-ko*   7個 *nana-ko*
2個 *ni-ko*   5個 *go-ko*   8個 *hak-ko*
3個 *san-ko*   6個 *rok-ko*   9個 *kyū-ko*
                                10個 *ju-ko*

本 **Hon** – This is the counter for long and stick-like objects that I've been referring to. Everything from ties, shoelaces, pens, spoons, forks, fluorescent lamps and even roads are counted with *hon*.

1本 *ip-pon*   4本 *yon-hon*   7本 *nana-hon*
2本 *ni-hon*   5本 *go-hon*   8本 *hap-pon*
3本 *sam-bon* 6本 *rop-pon*   9本 *kyū-hon*
                               10本 *jip-pon*

足 **Soku** – Counter for pairs of shoes and other footwear (including socks). Note that one pair, eight pairs and ten pairs are the result of sound changes in Japanese, so they're not *ichi-soku*, *hachi-soku* and *jū-soku*.

1足 *is-soku*   4足 *shi-soku*   7足 *nana-soku*
2足 *ni-soku*   5足 *go-soku*   8足 *has-soku*
3足 *san-soku* 6足 *roku-soku* 9足 *kyū-soku*
                                 10足 *jus-soku*

Example phrases

1. 1個の帽子
   ik-ko no bōshi
   one hat

2. 3枚のセーター
   san-mai no sētā
   three jumpers/sweaters

3. 4本のネクタイ
   yon-hon no nekutai
   four ties

4. 5足の靴下
   go-soku no kutsu-shita
   five pairs of socks

Quiz

You should be used to these by now (or sick of them!) Can you figure out what this person is trying to buy?

こんにちは！黒い手袋2枚、赤いジャケットを1枚買いたいです。
Konnichiwa! Kuroi te-bukuro ni-mai, akai jaketto o ichi-mai kaitai desu.

So, how was today's shopping? Did you get what you wanted?

Tomorrow is the final day of this book's program. We will wrap things up with loads of very useful, example phrases that you can keep practising past the 7th day mark. Tomorrow's lesson, I think, is the simplest of all because there is no grammar, yet what you learn tomorrow may possibly be the most useful going forward. I'll tell you why that is then because you must be tired from today's shopping. *O-yasumi-nasai.*

CHAPTER 7
ESSENTIAL PHRASES

Today is the last day of these lessons. Unlike in previous lessons the following phrases can be used in any situation and will be very useful when you want to let the other person know you are not a fluent speaker of Japanese, or you want to ask them to repeat what they just said but more slowly.

Most of them are stock phrases, and we won't be discussing grammar on our last day. Although I have tried to avoid using rote memorization throughout this book, there is simply no way to get around these common phrases. Learning them by heart is essential. They will be your convenient, go-to phrases that you can fall back on when you run out of Japanese words.

TELLING PEOPLE YOU DON'T SPEAK JAPANESE

1. すみません。日本語が話せません。
   Sumimasen. Nihon-go ga hanasemasen.
   I'm sorry. I can't speak Japanese.

2. 私は少し日本語が話せます。
   Watashi wa sukoshi Nihon-go ga hanasemasu.
   I can speak a little Japanese.

3. すみません。分かりません。
   Sumimasen. Wakarimasen.
   I'm sorry. I don't understand.

4. 英語が話せますか？
   Eigo ga hasemasu ka?
   Can you speak English?

5. 英語で説明してもらってもいいですか？
   Eigo de setsumei shite moratte mo ī desu ka?
   Can you explain that in English?

6. 書いてもらってもいいですか？
   Kaite moratte mo ī desu ka?
   Can you write that down?

7. これはどういう意味ですか？
   Kore wa dō iu imi desu ka?
   What does this mean?

ASKING PEOPLE TO REPEAT THEMSELVES

8. すみません。聞き取れませんでした。
   Sumimasen. Kikitoremasen deshita.
   I'm sorry. I didn't catch that.

9. もう一度（ゆっくり）言ってください。
   Mō ichido (yukkuri) itte kudasai.
   Please say that again (slowly)?

10. 翻訳アプリにもう一度言ってもらってもいいですか？
    Hon'yaku apuri ni mō ichido itte moratte mo ī desu ka?
    Can I ask you to repeat that to a translation app?

ASKING PEOPLE FOR HELP

11. ちょっと手伝ってくれませんか？
    Chotto te-tsudatte kuremasen ka?
    Can you help me?

12. ちょっといいですか？
    Chotto ī desu ka?
    Can I have a minute?

13. ちょっと聞いてもいいですか？
    Chotto kīte mo ī desu ka?
    Can I ask you something?

14. これは何ですか？
    Kore wa nan desu ka?
    What is this?

15. これは何と言いますか？
    Kore wa nan to īmasu ka?
    What do you call this?

16. これはいくらですか？
    Kore wa ikura desu ka?
    How much is this?

17. …はどこですか？
    …wa doko desu ka?
    Where is…?

18. この辺でお勧めの観光スポットはありますか？

    Kono hen de o-susume no kankō supotto wa arimasu ka?

    Are there any tourist spots that you can recommend around here?

AGREEING AND DISAGREEING

19. はい、そうです。

    Hai, sō desu.

    Yes, that's it.

20. いいえ、違います。

    Īe, chigaimasu.

    No, that's not it.

21. これが好きです。

    Kore ga suki desu.

    I like this.

22. これが好きじゃないです。

    Kore ga suki ja nai desu.

    I don't like this.

ENDING THE CONVERSATION

23. はい、分かりました。ありがとう（ございます）。
    Hai, wakarimashita. Arigatō (gozaimasu).
    Yes, got it. (I understood you.) Thank you.

24. そろそろ行きます。／そろそろ帰ります。
    Sorosoro ikimasu./Sorosoro kaerimasu.
    I am leaving soon./I am going home soon.

25. 助けていただきありがとう（ございます）。
    Tasukete itadaki arigatō (gozaimasu).
    Thanks for helping me.

26. お話できてよかったです！
    O-hanashi dekite yokatta!
    It was nice talking with you!

27. またすぐにお話しましょう！
    Mata sugu ni o-hanashimasho!
    Talk to you soon!

Quiz

Finally, figure out what this person has just asked. It may seem like a lot but take your time and do your best!

1. こんばんは、手伝ってもらってもいいですか？私は少し日本語が話せます。この辺でお勧めの観光スポットはありますか？もう一度ゆっくり言ってください。

    Konnichiwa, te-tsudatte moratte mo ī desu ka? Watashi wa sukoshi Nihon-go ga hanasemasu. Kono hen de o-susume no kankō supotto wa arimasu ka? Mō ichido yukkuri itte kudasai.

ANSWER SHEET TO QUIZZES

CHAPTER 1 (GREETINGS)

"Good morning! Nice to meet you, my name is John, where are you from?"

CHAPTER 2 (BASIC VOCABULARY)

"The time is half past 8 in the morning. It looks like it is going to rain tomorrow. What is the weather forecast for the weekend?"

CHAPTER 3 (TRAVELLING & PLACES)

"Where is the nearest station? How many minutes will it take to go to the station by foot?"

CHAPTER 4 (FAMILY & RELATIONSHIPS)

"I have one older brother and two younger sisters. My brother's name is Peter. He is 30 years old."

CHAPTER 5 (FOOD & EATING OUT)

"Excuse me. Could I please have a coffee with milk to drink, bread to start then sushi for my main course?"

CHAPTER 6 (SHOPPING & CLOTHES)

"Hello! I would like to buy 2 pairs of black gloves and 1 red jacket."

CHAPTER 7 (USEFUL PHRASES)

"Good evening. Can you help me? I speak a little Japanese. Are there any tourist spots that you can recommend around here? Could you repeat that more slowly?"

CONCLUSION

By no means are you expected to have mastered the language or gained fluency at this point. I'm sure many of the things we've discussed in the past week are still mysterious or confusing. This is totally natural when learning a new language. Both children and language majors alike take years to gain fluency.

It may be frustrating, but the key is to just keep pushing until you reach that critical mass when everything suddenly starts to make sense. You will still learn new things every day after that point, but they should start to flow more easily because you can connect them with past concepts—the foundations—that you have learned.

I know we kept hammering in this book how Japanese has different polite forms for verbs and nouns, but you don't even need to master these to have a basic, conversational understanding of Japanese. Those complexities will fix themselves as your skills level up in the future. We touched upon politeness, counter words and so on because those are things people will use when they speak with you. They will be polite with you even if you aren't (unintentionally, I hope!). They will use the correct counter words with you even if the only way to count that you know is *hito-tsu*, *futa-tsu* and so on. Long story short, you should know that these complexities exist, but you should not be frustrated that you can't wrap your head around them just yet.

Going forward, my suggestion is that you expand your vocabulary gradually every day. Try learning 5 to 10 new words a day, starting with the most basic. Things that you can find in your house for example. So that, by the end of the month, you can name almost everything you own. Techniques like this do help. As well as that, try to start memorizing both *hiragana* and *katakana* and the more basic *kanji*. Writing them down will help massively.

Dealing with grammar is a little bit trickier, but I find that encountering lots of example sentences and then noticing the patterns naturally is a less daunting task for beginner students than discussing grammatical concepts in depth and then later applying them. At any rate, you can further research grammatical concepts whenever you are curious or whenever there are grey areas that you would like to clear up.

The key here is to make your study bite-sized, so that your expectations are realistic, and you then feel rewarded at the end of the day and have the willingness to keep moving forward.

This goes back to my philosophy in writing this book. What I would like you to take away are some of the more common words and the most basic sentence structures that you will immediately find useful when talking to Japanese people even if your Japanese is ungrammatical or "broken," so to speak.

Lastly, go out and practise! If you know any people who speak Japanese, great! If not, use the Internet and social media. You will find that these can be very useful tools for practising Japanese and making Japanese friends online. Either way, offline or online, I would encourage you to find friends that you can chat with in Japanese. I promise you your language skills will improve beyond your expectation!

I hope you found the Japanese language as fascinating as it is complex. If you enjoyed this book and found it helpful, please leave a review on Amazon. I'll read all your comments, and I would genuinely welcome feedback on how I can improve this book, so that more people can appreciate the beauty of the language and culture that you and I love.

Printed in Great Britain
by Amazon